AF408346

# *Divine Timeless Secrets In the Amazing Story of Musa and Khidr*

Dr. Muddassir Khan

In the Name of Allah, The Most Merciful,
The Bestower of Mercy.

# Table of Contents

# Introduction

The story of Prophet Moses (Musa) and al-Khidr (peace be upon them both) is mentioned in detail in the verses in Surah al-Kahf and also in the lengthy hadeeth narrated by Imam al-Bukhaari (no. 3401) and Imam Muslim (no. 2380).

Many amazing lessons, reminders, and benefits are present in this story. This book will try to derive these lessons based on an authentic explanation of the Quran and the Hadeeth. By reading this book you will learn numerous impactful lessons that will change your way of thinking and help you start your journey towards becoming a righteous Muslim in search of beneficial knowledge.

# Verse 60

وَإِذ

And when

قَالَ

said

مُوسَىٰ

Musa

لِفَتَـٰهُ

to his boy,

لَآ

"Not

أَبْرَحُ

I will cease

حَتَّىٰٓ

until

أَبْلُغَ

I reach

مَجْمَعَ

the junction

ٱلْبَحْرَيْنِ

(of) the two seas

أَوْ

or

أَمْضِيَ

I continue

حُقُبًا

(for) a long period."
60

$$\text{وَإِذْ قَالَ مُوسَىٰ لِفَتَىٰهُ لَآ أَبْرَحُ حَتَّىٰٓ}$$

$$\text{أَبْلُغَ مَجْمَعَ ٱلْبَحْرَيْنِ أَوْ أَمْضِىَ}$$

$$\text{حُقُبًا ﴿٦٠﴾ [الكهف: 60]}$$

«And [mention] when Moses said to his servant, "I will not cease [traveling] until I reach the junction of the two seas or continue for a long period." (60) »
[Al-Kahf: 60]

## Narration of the Prophet (peace and blessings of Allah be upon him)

It is narrated in Sahih al-Bukhari that the Prophet (ﷺ) said (combined narrations):

$$\text{أَنَّ مُوسَى قَامَ خَطِيبًا فِي بَنِي إِسْرَائِيل}$$

Once Moses stood up and addressed Bani Israel.

فَسُئِلَ أَيُّ النَّاسِ أَعْلَمُ فَقَالَ أَنَا

He was then asked about who was the most learned man amongst the people. He (Moses) said, 'I'. (Moses was not aware of other messengers at his time, so he said that he is the most knowledgeable man)

فَعَتَبَ اللَّهُ عَلَيْهِ إِذْ لَمْ يَرُدَّ الْعِلْمَ إِلَيْهِ.

Allah then admonished him (censured Moses for not entrusting the knowledge of this affair, that is about who is the most knowledgeable man, to Allah) since he did not attribute absolute knowledge to Him (that is Allah. Moses should have said that Allah knows best).

فَقَالَ لَهُ بَلَى، لِي عَبْدٌ بِمَجْمَعِ الْبَحْرَيْنِ هُوَ أَعْلَمُ مِنْكَ

Then Allah said to him, 'Yes, there is a Slave of Mine at the junction of the two seas who is more learned than you.'

Moses asked (Allah), 'O my Lord! How can I meet him (the slave of Allah who is more knowledgeable than Moses)?

قَالَ تَأْخُذُ حُوتًا، فَتَجْعَلُهُ فِي مِكْتَلٍ، حَيْثُمَا فَقَدْتَ الْحُوتَ فَهْوَ ثَمَّ ـ وَرُبَّمَا قَالَ فَهْوَ ثَمَّهْ

Allah said, 'Take a fish and put it in a large basket and you will find him (the slave of Allah who is more knowledgeable than you) at the place where you will lose the fish.'

وَأَخَذَ حُوتًا، فَجَعَلَهُ فِي مِكْتَلٍ، ثُمَّ انْطَلَقَ هُوَ وَفَتَاهُ يُوشَعُ بْنُ نُونٍ

Moses took a fish and put it in a basket and proceeded along with his (servant) boy, Yusha` bin Nun

فَقَالَ لِفَتَاهُ لاَ أُكَلِّفُكَ إِلاَّ أَنْ تُخْبِرَنِي بِحَيْثُ يُفَارِقُكَ الْحُوتُ. قَالَ مَا كَلَّفْتَ كَثِيرًا

Then Moses said to his boy-servant "I don't want to trouble you, except that you should inform me as soon as this fish leaves you." He said (to Moses): "You have not demanded too much."

*This narration of the Prophet (peace and blessings of Allah be upon him) will be continued simultaneously along with the explanation of the verses of the Quran.*

## Explanation of the verse

وَإِذْ قَالَ مُوسَىٰ لِفَتَـٰهُ

And (mention) when Moses said to his servant
(Yusha bin Nun)

The reason for Moses's (peace be upon him) conversation with the boy, Yusha 'bin Nun (as mentioned in this verse), was because he had been told about one of Allah's servants at the junction of the two seas, who had knowledge that Moses had not been given, so he wanted to travel to meet him and take knowledge from him. Moses (peace be upon him) said to this boy-servant of his:

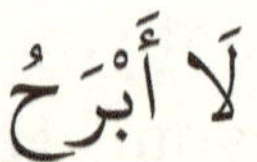

(I will not give up) which means, I will keep on traveling,

$$\text{حَتَّىٰ أَبْلُغَ مَجْمَعَ الْبَحْرَيْنِ}$$

(until I reach the junction of the two seas) meaning, the place where the two seas meet.

$$\text{أَوْ أَمْضِيَ حُقُبًا}$$

(or a *Huqub* passes.)

Which means, even in case I have to travel a very long time (I will keep on traveling to meet this slave of Allah). Ibn Jarir (Allah have mercy on him) said: "Some of the scholars of the Arabic language said that *Huqub* means a year...". 'Abdullah bin' Amr said: "*Huqub* means eighty years." Mujahid said, "Seventy years." 'Ali bin Abi Talhah reported that Ibn' Abbas said that it means a lifetime. Qatadah and Ibn Zayd said the same thing. This shows the longing, unwavering resolve, and eagerness of Moses which made him say these things to his servant.

This also shows the great eagerness and determination of Prophet Moses (Musa – peace be upon him) to pursue goodness and seek knowledge. He said to his servant, who was constantly by his side at home and on the journey, whose name was Yusha ibn Nun, to whom Allah subsequently blessed with Prophethood. Moses clarified everything to his servant-boy so that there is no confusion and their travel together will be easy.

لَا أَبْرَحُ حَتَّى أَبْلُغَ مَجْمَعَ الْبَحْرَيْنِ

I won't give up until I reach the junction of the two seas.

Moses was determined to carry on traveling even if this causes lengthy hardships and even if he became exhausted until he reaches his destination (the junction of the two seas and the place where the dead fish will come alive and he will lose the fish). In this place as mentioned in the narration of the Prophet (peace and blessings of Allah be upon him), he would find one of the knowledgeable slaves of Allah who had been given the knowledge that Moses did not possess.

Al-Qurtubi says that in this event of Moses traveling to gain knowledge there is the wisdom of scholarly travels in order to increase one's knowledge. It also includes the principle of taking help from a servant or companion is such an endeavor instead of going on one's own. The verse also points to the importance of seizing the opportunities to meet noble souls and eminent scholars, even though their abodes are far away. This was a common practice among the previous generations of righteous scholars. Al-Bukhaaree mentioned that the Companion Jaabir ibn 'Abdillaah (Allah be pleased with him) traveled a month's journey to obtain a single *hadith* from another Companion, 'Abdullaah ibn Unays (Allah be pleased with him).

Musa (peace be upon him) was dedicated to acquiring knowledge. He was in no way proud of what he knows. Musa was one of the great Messengers of Allah but that did not stop him from learning from Khidr (the slave of Allah). To gain knowledge Musa had to travel. This shows that a person needs to struggle to gain knowledge. We should take a lesson from this incident and not be shy to learn from even someone who is younger than us. We should increase our knowledge. Musa (peace be upon him) had knowledge but wanted to increase in it. There is no limit to knowledge.

فَلَمَّا

But when

بَلَغَا

they reached

مَجْمَعَ

the junction

بَيْنِهِمَا

between them,

نَسِيَا

they forgot

حُوتَهُمَا

their fish,

فَٱتَّخَذَ

and it took

سَبِيلَهُۥ

its way

فِى

into

ٱلْبَحْرِ

the sea,

سَرَبًا

slipping away.

61

$$\text{فَلَمَّا بَلَغَا مَجْمَعَ بَيْنِهِمَا نَسِيَا}$$

$$\text{حُوتَهُمَا فَاتَّخَذَ سَبِيلَهُ فِي ٱلْبَحْرِ}$$

$$\text{سَرَبًا ﴿٦١﴾ [الكهف: 61]}$$

«But when they reached the junction between them, they forgot their fish, and it took its course into the sea, slipping away (61) » [Al-Kahf: 61]

**Continuation of the Narration of the Prophet (peace and blessings of Allah be upon him)**

$$\text{وَأَخَذَ حُوتًا، فَجَعَلَهُ فِي مِكْتَلٍ، ثُمَّ انْطَلَقَ هُوَ وَفَتَاهُ}$$

$$\text{يُوشَعُ بْنُ نُونٍ، حَتَّى أَتَيَا الصَّخْرَةَ، وَضَعَا رُءُوسَهُمَا}$$

$$\text{فَرَقَدَ مُوسَى}$$

Moses took a fish and put it in a basket and proceeded along with his (servant) boy, Yusha`bin

Nun, till they reached the rock where they laid their heads (i.e., lay down). Moses slept

وَاضْطَرَبَ الْحُوتُ فَخَرَجَ فَسَقَطَ فِي الْبَحْرِ، فَاتَّخَذَ سَبِيلَهُ فِي الْبَحْرِ سَرَبًا، فَأَمْسَكَ اللَّهُ عَنِ الْحُوتِ جِرْيَةَ الْمَاءِ، فَصَارَ مِثْلَ الطَّاقِ، فَقَالَ هَكَذَا مِثْلُ الطَّاقِ.

the fish, moving out of the basket, fell into the sea. It took its way into the sea (straight) as in a tunnel. Allah stopped the flow of water over the fish and it became like an arch [the Prophet (ﷺ) pointed out this arch with his hands].

فَبَيْنَمَا هُوَ فِي ظِلِّ صَخْرَةٍ فِي مَكَانٍ ثَرْيَانَ، إِذْ تَضَرَّبَ الْحُوتُ، وَمُوسَى نَائِمٌ، فَقَالَ فَتَاهُ لاَ أُوقِظُهُ حَتَّى إِذَا اسْتَيْقَظَ نَسِيَ أَنْ يُخْبِرَهُ

While the attendant (Yusha) was in the shade of the rock at a wet place, the fish slipped out (alive) while Moses was sleeping. His attendant said (to himself), "I will not wake him", but when he (Moses) woke up, he (Yusha) forgot to inform him.

# Explanation of verse 61

فَلَمَّا بَلَغَا مَجْمَعَ بَيْنِهِمَا نَسِيَا حُوتَهُمَا

*(But when they reached the junction of the two seas, they forgot their fish,)*

Moses (peace be upon him) had been commanded to carry a salted fish with him, and it had been said to him that when he loses the fish, it will be a sign that he has reached his destination. Here they would find the slave of Allah for whom they were looking. So, they (Moses and Yusha) set out and traveled until they reached the junction between the two seas. They lay down to sleep there, and the fish came to life. It was in a vessel with Yusha (peace be upon him) and it jumped out of the vessel towards the sea. Yusha woke up and the fish fell into the water and began to swim through the water, leaving a trail or channel behind. The fish making its way into the sea was one of the signs. The first sign was when the two seas came together and the second sign is when they lose the fish. They missed the sign since Musa (peace be upon him) slept and though Yusha (peace be upon him) saw it he forgot to mention it to Musa.

فَاتَّخَذَ سَبِيلَهُ فِي الْبَحْرِ سَرَبًا

Which means it went like it was going through a tunnel on land. Ibn 'Abbas said, 'It left a trace (in the water) as if it were a rock.'

The sea parted when the fish exited the basket and entered the sea, and it began to swim in the sea. Normally when the fish swims in the sea, the water covers it. However, this was a sign from Allah, and the water split and it did not settle. This was a dead fish that came to life and then took this path, and this is from the signs of Allah.

# Verse 62

فَلَمَّا

Then when

جَاوَزَا

they had passed beyond

قَالَ

he said

لِفَتَـٰهُ

to his boy,

ءَاتِنَا

"Bring us

غَدَآءَنَا

our morning meal.

لَقَدْ

Certainly

لَقِينَا

we have suffered

مِن

in

سَفَرِنَا

our journey

هَـٰذَا

this,

نَصَبًا

fatigue."
62

فَلَمَّا جَاوَزَا قَالَ لِفَتَاهُ ءَاتِنَا غَدَآءَنَا لَقَدْ لَقِينَا مِن سَفَرِنَا هَاذَا نَصَبًا ﴿٦٢﴾

[الكهف: 62]

«So when they had passed beyond it, [Moses] said to his boy, "Bring us our morning meal. We have certainly suffered in this, our journey, [much] fatigue."(62)» [Al-Kahf: 62]

**Continuation of the Narration of the Prophet (peace and blessings of Allah be upon him)**

فَانْطَلَقَا يَمْشِيَانِ بَقِيَّةَ لَيْلَتِهِمَا وَيَوْمَهُمَا، حَتَّى إِذَا كَانَ مِنَ الْغَدِ قَالَ لِفَتَاهُ

They traveled the rest of the night, and the next day Moses said to his boy (servant),

آتِنَا غَدَاءَنَا لَقَدْ لَقِينَا مِنْ سَفَرِنَا هَذَا نَصَبًا.

'Give us our food, for indeed, we have suffered much fatigue in this journey of ours.'

وَلَمْ يَجِدْ مُوسَى النَّصَبَ حَتَّى جَاوَزَ حَيْثُ أَمَرَهُ اللَّهُ.

Moses did not feel tired till he crossed that place which Allah had ordered him to seek after.

## Explanation of the Verse

قَالَ لِفَتَاهُ آتِنَا غَدَاءَنَا لَقَدْ لَقِينَا مِن سَفَرِنَا هَٰذَا

([Moses] said to his boy-servant: "Bring us our morning meal; truly, we have suffered in this, our journey)

This means their journey beyond the place where they should have stopped. They had become tired, and their tiredness only began when they had missed their destination. They did not feel tired before they came to the junction between the two seas. This was one of the signs that indicated to Moses that what he was seeking for was here. His longing to reach the place of his destination had made the traveling easy but when he went beyond the destination (the place where they had lost the fish and where they would find Khidr), he began to feel tired. So, Moses (peace be upon him) wanted to eat.

نَصَبًا

(Nasaban) means, exhaustion.

Their tiredness and exhaustion immediately on missing their destination was a sign from Allah. This was so they would not walk far from the place where Khidr was located. Allah caused Prophet Moses to become weary and tired.

Moses asked for his lunch to eat. He had carried provisions and supplies before starting to travel. This is from the *Tawakkul* (reliance) on Allah that you carry out the means and also place your *Tawakkul* on Allah. It is wrong to start a major journey without taking provisions claiming that you are trusting Allah. The Prophet of Allah - Moses (peace be upon him) took provisions with him even though he had complete trust (*Tawakkul*) in Allah.

There were some people from Yemen who used to do Hajj without taking provisions with them. They said, "We are those who truly trust in Allah." But because of this when they came to Makkah, they would beg people. Therefore, Allah revealed the verse:

ٱلۡحَجُّ أَشۡهُرٞ مَّعۡلُومَٰتٞۚ فَمَن فَرَضَ فِيهِنَّ ٱلۡحَجَّ فَلَا رَفَثَ وَلَا فُسُوقَ وَلَا جِدَالَ فِي ٱلۡحَجِّۗ وَمَا تَفۡعَلُواْ مِنۡ خَيۡرٖ يَعۡلَمۡهُ ٱللَّهُۗ وَتَزَوَّدُواْ فَإِنَّ خَيۡرَ ٱلزَّادِ ٱلتَّقۡوَىٰۚ وَٱتَّقُونِ يَٰٓأُوْلِي ٱلۡأَلۡبَٰبِ ۝١٩٧ [البقرة: 197]

«Hajj is [during] well-known months, so whoever has made Hajj obligatory upon himself therein [by entering the state of ihram], there is [to be for him] no sexual relations and no disobedience and no disputing during Hajj. And whatever good you do - Allah knows it. **And take provisions (for the journey), but indeed, the best provision is**

**fear of Allah. And fear Me, O you of understanding (197) » [Al-Baqara: 197]**

$$\text{لَقَدْ لَقِينَا مِن سَفَرِنَا هَٰذَا نَصَبًا}$$

Moses said, "Indeed we have suffered much fatigue in this journey of ours." This shows that we can inform others about our suffering or sickness (without being angry or distressed) and this does not contradict *ridaa* (being pleased with one's destiny).

# Verse 63

قَالَ

He said,

أَرَءَيْتَ

"Did you see,

إِذْ

when

أَوَيْنَآ

we retired

إِلَى

to

ٱلصَّخْرَةِ

the rock?

فَإِنِّى

Then indeed, I

نَسِيتُ

[I] forgot

ٱلْحُوتَ

the fish.

وَمَآ

And not

أَنْسَٰنِيهُ

made me forget it

إِلَّا

except

ٱلشَّيْطَٰنُ

the Shaitaan

أَنْ

that

أَذْكُرَهُ

I mention it.

وَٱتَّخَذَ

And it took

سَبِيلَهُ

its way

فِى

into

ٱلْبَحْرِ

the sea

عَجَبًا

amazingly."

قَالَ أَرَءَيْتَ إِذْ أَوَيْنَآ إِلَى ٱلصَّخْرَةِ فَإِنِّى نَسِيتُ ٱلْحُوتَ وَمَآ أَنسَىٰنِيهُ إِلَّا ٱلشَّيْطَٰنُ أَنْ أَذْكُرَهُۥ وَٱتَّخَذَ سَبِيلَهُۥ فِى ٱلْبَحْرِ عَجَبًا ۝ [الكهف: 63]

«He said, "Did you see when we retired to the rock? Indeed, I forgot [there] the fish. And none made me forget it except Satan - that I should mention it. And it

# took its course into the sea amazingly" (63) » [Al-Kahf: 63]

## Continuation of the Narration of the Prophet (peace and blessings of Allah be upon him)

قَالَ لَهُ فَتَاهُ أَرَأَيْتَ إِذْ أَوَيْنَا إِلَى الصَّخْرَةِ فَإِنِّي نَسِيتُ الْحُوتَ، وَمَا أَنْسَانِيهِ إِلاَّ الشَّيْطَانُ أَنْ أَذْكُرَهُ، وَاتَّخَذَ سَبِيلَهُ فِي الْبَحْرِ عَجَبًا، فَكَانَ لِلْحُوتِ سَرَبًا وَلَهُمَا عَجَبًا.

His boy (servant) said to him, 'Do you know that when we were sitting near that rock, I forgot the fish, and none but Shaitan caused me to forget to tell (you) about it, and it took its course into the sea in an amazing way?.' So there was a path for the fish and that astonished them.

## Explanation of the verse

قَالَ أَرَأَيْتَ إِذْ أَوَيْنَا إِلَى الصَّخْرَةِ فَإِنِّي نَسِيتُ الْحُوتَ
وَمَا أَنْسَانِيهُ إِلَّا الشَّيْطَانُ أَنْ أَذْكُرَهُ

He (Yusha) said: "Do you remember when we betook ourselves to the rock? I indeed forgot the fish; none but Shaytan made me forget to remember it..." Then he said,

وَاتَّخَذَ سَبِيلَهُ

'It took its course', meaning its path,

فِي الْبَحْرِ عَجَبًا

"...into the sea in a strange (way)!"

Yusha (peace be upon him) asked Musa in amazement, "Do you remember?" Yusha (peace be upon him) admitted that he forgot to mention to Moses (peace be upon him) about the amazing incident of the fish and it was the Shaitan who had caused him to forget. He told Moses (peace be upon him) that this incident had happened when they had stopped for the night besides that well-known rock, which was between the two seas.

This incident shows that forgetfulness is acceptable and such forgetfulness happens to humans. Shaitan causes humans to forget their important duties and indulge in other things. We sometimes know things but we forget. We should not assume the worst and say to others, 'no you did not forget'. We should not scold others otherwise we will not go forward on the path to seeking knowledge. We should therefore overlook and pardon.

Yusha (peace be upon him) was amazed by the fish since this fish would pass by water and leave a path in the water like a tunnel. This is an amazing miracle since water normally covers what passes through it, but, by the permission of Allah, the water did not cover this fish.

This incident of forgetting also shows that shaitan wants to delay you and make your path to knowledge and guidance longer. Shaitan is your enemy and he never wants you to reach your destination. Forgetfulness is one of the main tools used by Shaitan to misguide humans.

Allah says in the Quran:

ٱسۡتَحۡوَذَ عَلَيۡهِمُ ٱلشَّيۡطَـٰنُ فَأَنسَـٰهُمۡ

ذِكۡرَ ٱللَّهِ أُوْلَـٰٓئِكَ حِزۡبُ ٱلشَّيۡطَـٰنِ أَلَآ

$$\text{إِنَّ حِزْبَ ٱلشَّيْطَانِ هُمُ}$$

$$\text{ٱلْخَاسِرُونَ ﴿١٩﴾}$$ [المجادلة: 19]

«Satan has overcome them and made them forget the remembrance of Allah. Those are the party of Satan. Unquestionably, the party of Satan - they will be the losers (19) » [Al-Mujadila: 19]

The Muslim is encouraged to regularly remember Allah as much as possible. Sin is generally committed when Allah is forgotten. Shaitan seeks to occupy a person's mind with irrelevant thoughts and wants to make him forget Allah. Once Allah is forgotten a person willingly joins the party of Shaitan.

# Verse 64

قَالَ

He said,

ذَٰلِكَ

"That

مَا

(is) what

كُنَّا

we were

نَبْغِ

seeking."

فَٱرْتَدَّا

So they returned

عَلَىٰٓ

on

ءَاثَارِهِمَا

their footprints,

قَصَصًا

retracing.

64

$$\text{قَالَ ذَٰلِكَ مَا كُنَّا نَبْغِ فَٱرْتَدَّا عَلَىٰٓ}$$

$$\text{ءَاثَارِهِمَا قَصَصًا ۝ } \quad \text{[الكهف: 64]}$$

«[Moses] said, "That is what we were seeking." So they returned, following their footprints (64) » [Al-Kahf: 64]

## Continuation of the Narration of the Prophet (peace and blessings of Allah be upon him)

$$\text{قَالَ لَهُ مُوسَى ذَلِكَ مَا كُنَّا نَبْغِي، فَارْتَدَّا عَلَى آثَارِهِمَا}$$

$$\text{قَصَصًا، رَجَعَا يَقُصَّانِ آثَارَهُمَا حَتَّى انْتَهَيَا إِلَى}$$

$$\text{الصَّخْرَةِ}$$

Moses said, 'That was what we were seeking after.' So, both of them retraced their footsteps till they reached the rock.

## Explanation of the verse:

قَالَ ذَٰلِكَ مَا كُنَّا نَبْغِ

[Moses] said: "That is what we have been seeking."

He meant this is what we have been looking for.

فَارْتَدَّا

So they went back

عَلَىٰ آثَارِهِمَا

their footsteps.

Moses told Yusha that what he just said was exactly the sign they were looking for. They, therefore, returned back after traveling a tiresome distance since this was the place where they will meet al-Khidr.

Moses (peace be upon him) did not ask Yusha (peace be upon him) as to how he could forget. He reminded him that this was the sign they were seeking and went back retracing their footsteps so that they would not miss the place where they had rested. Seeking knowledge is worship and searching for knowledge is also worship, and nothing goes to waste with Allah when a person does a righteous action with the correct intention.

# Verse 65

فَوَجَدَا

Then they found

عَبْدًا

a servant

مِّنْ

from

عِبَادِنَآ

Our servants,

ءَاتَيْنَـٰهُ

whom We had given

رَحْمَةً

mercy

مِّنْ

from

عِندِنَا

Us,

وَعَلَّمْنَـٰهُ

and We had taught him

مِن

from

لَّدُنَّا

Us

عِلْمًا

a knowledge.

65

فَوَجَدَا عَبْدًا مِّنْ عِبَادِنَآ ءَاتَيْنَـٰهُ
رَحْمَةً مِّنْ عِندِنَا وَعَلَّمْنَـٰهُ مِن لَّدُنَّا
عِلْمًا ﴿٦٥﴾ [الكهف: 65]

«And they found a servant from among Our servants to whom we had given mercy from us and had taught him from Us a [certain] knowledge (65) » [Al-Kahf: 65]

## Continuation of the Narration of the Prophet (peace and blessings of Allah be upon him)

فَإِذَا رَجُلٌ مُسَجَّى بِثَوْبٍ، فَسَلَّمَ مُوسَى، فَرَدَّ عَلَيْهِ.
فَقَالَ وَأَنَّى بِأَرْضِكَ السَّلَامُ. قَالَ أَنَا مُوسَى. قَالَ
مُوسَى بَنِي إِسْرَائِيلَ قَالَ نَعَمْ،

There they saw a man Lying covered with a garment. Moses greeted him (saying As-salaam alaykum) and he replied saying, 'How do people greet each other in your land?' Moses said, 'I am Moses.' The man asked, 'Moses of Bani Israel?' Moses said, 'Yes,

## Explanation of the Verse

فَوَجَدَا عَبْدًا مِّنْ عِبَادِنَا آتَيْنَاهُ رَحْمَةً مِّنْ عِندِنَا
وَعَلَّمْنَاهُ مِن لَّدُنَّا عِلْمًا

Then they found one of Our servants, on whom We had bestowed mercy from Us, and whom We had taught knowledge from Us.

The person they found was Al-Khidr, peace be upon him, as is indicated by the authentic narration of the Messenger of Allah ﷺ.

Al-Khidr (peace be upon him) is one of the slaves of Allah and his student is Moses (peace be upon him) who was a Messenger of Determination (strong resolve). Allah had granted Khidr special mercy through which his knowledge increased and he did righteous deeds.

Although Moses had more knowledge than Khidr in most matters of faith and the fundamentals of laws and regulations, Khidr was given knowledge by Allah that had not been given to Moses. This knowledge as we come to know in their story is the knowledge of the unseen. This knowledge was based on things that would occur in the future and was something from the unseen. Prophet Moses (peace be upon him) was a high-ranking Prophet and wanted to derive the benefit from this distinguished knowledge of Khidr, and for this very purpose, he had undertaken this journey.

# Verse 66

قَالَ

Said

لَهُ

to him

مُوسَىٰ

Musa,

هَلْ

"May,

أَتَّبِعُكَ

I follow you

عَلَىٰٓ

on

أَن

that

تُعَلِّمَنِ

you teach me

مِمَّا

of what

عُلِّمْتَ

you have been taught

رُشْدًا

## (of) right guidance?"

## 66

قَالَ لَهُۥ مُوسَىٰ هَلۡ أَتَّبِعُكَ عَلَىٰٓ أَن تُعَلِّمَنِ مِمَّا عُلِّمۡتَ رُشۡدًا ۝ [الكهف: 66]

«Moses said to him, "May I follow you on [the condition] that you teach me from what you have been taught of sound judgement?" (66) » [Al-Kahf: 66]

**Continuation of the Narration of the Prophet (peace and blessings of Allah be upon him)**

أَتَيْتُكَ لِتُعَلِّمَنِي مِمَّا عُلِّمْتَ رَشَدًا. قَالَ يَا مُوسَى إِنِّي عَلَى عِلْمٍ مِنْ عِلْمِ اللَّهِ، عَلَّمَنِيهِ اللَّهُ لاَ تَعْلَمُهُ وَأَنْتَ عَلَى عِلْمٍ مِنْ عِلْمِ اللَّهِ عَلَّمَكَهُ اللَّهُ لاَ أَعْلَمُهُ.

(Moses said) 'I have come to you so that you may teach me from those things which Allah has taught you.' He said, 'O Moses! I have some of the Knowledge of Allah which Allah has taught me, and which you do not know, while you have some of the Knowledge of Allah which Allah has taught you and which I do not know.'

قَالَ هَلْ أَتَّبِعُكَ

Moses asked, 'May I follow you?'

**Explanation of the Verse:**

قَالَ لَهُ مُوسَىٰ هَلْ أَتَّبِعُكَ

Moses said to him: "May I follow you..."

This is a question formulated in gentle terms, with no sense of power or coercion. This is the way in which the seeker of knowledge should approach the scholar.

أَتَّبِعُكَ

'I follow you' means that I (Moses) accompany you (Khidr) and spend time with you.

عَلَىٰ أَن تُعَلِّمَنِ مِمَّا عُلِّمْتَ رُشْدًا

'so that you teach me something of that knowledge which you have been taught'.

This means that you teach me something of what Allah has taught you so that I can be guided by it and learn something beneficial and do righteous actions.

Moses (peace be upon him) showed much respect to Al-Khidr (peace be upon him) even though Moses was a great Messenger of Allah. This was because Khidr was his teacher and therefore he presented his request to him politely seeking his consent. This shows the manners of a student to his teacher. It also shows the kindness and humility of Moses (peace be upon him). He asked him whether he can follow him on the basis that he teaches him some of the sound knowledge that Allah has taught him. We also learn from this story that we need to get the knowledge since knowledge does not come to us and we need to strive and go in search of knowledge. The student of knowledge much be humble, respectful, and kind with his teacher and should deal with him in an honorable manner.

The teacher and the one who is granted knowledge by Allah should be happy if he is given the opportunity to teach others and if knowledge is taken from him. The knowledge taken from a person during his lifetime will benefit him in the Hereafter.

The Prophet (peace and blessings of Allah be upon him) said:

إِذَا مَاتَ الإِنْسَانُ انْقَطَعَ عَنْهُ عَمَلُهُ إِلاَّ مِنْ ثَلاَثَةٍ إِلاَّ مِنْ صَدَقَةٍ جَارِيَةٍ أَوْ عِلْمٍ يُنْتَفَعُ بِهِ أَوْ وَلَدٍ صَالِحٍ يَدْعُو لَهُ

When a person dies, his acts come to an end, except three: recurring (ongoing) charity, **or knowledge (by which people) benefit**, or a pious (righteous) son, who prays for him (for the deceased).

قَالَ

He said,

إِنَّكَ

"Indeed, you

لَن

never

تَسْتَطِيعَ

will be able,

مَعِىَ

with me,

صَبْرًا

(to have) patience.

67

قَالَ إِنَّكَ لَن تَسْتَطِيعَ مَعِيَ صَبْرًا ﴿٦٧﴾

[الكهف: 67]

«He said, "Indeed, with me you will never be able to have patience (67) » [Al-Kahf: 67]

## Explanation of the verse

In this verse, we find a very direct and straightforward response from Al-Khidr (peace be upon him) similar to the style of Moses (peace be upon him). Al-Khidr did not refuse the request of Moses but said that he (Moses) will never be able to have patience with him (Khidr). Moses will see things if he was to follow Khidr which will appear to be evil outwardly but inwardly will be otherwise. Moses will not be able to be patient seeing the extraordinary actions that Khidr had been ordered to do by Allah.  To gain knowledge a person should be patient. Patience is required when seeking knowledge and also after gaining knowledge.

وَكَيْفَ

And how can

تَصْبِرُ

you have patience

عَلَىٰ

for

مَا

what

لَمْ

ᵛnot

تُحِطْ

you encompass

بِهِۦ

of it

خُبْرًا

any knowledge."

68

وَكَيْفَ تَصْبِرُ عَلَىٰ مَا لَمْ تُحِطْ بِهِۦ خُبْرًا ۞ [الكهف: 68]

«And how can you have patience for what you do not encompass in knowledge?"(68)» [Al-Kahf: 68]

## Explanation of the Verse

$$\textarabic{قَالَ}$$

(He said) meaning, Al-Khidr (peace be upon him) said to Musa (peace be upon him),

$$\textarabic{إِنَّكَ لَن تَسْتَطِيعَ مَعِيَ صَبْرًا}$$

Verily, you will not be able to have patience with me!

This means, 'You will not be able to follow me when you see me do things that are contrary to your law because I have knowledge from Allah which He has not taught you and you have knowledge from Allah which He has not taught me. Each of us has a responsibility to Allah that the other does not share and you will not be able to stay with me'.

$$\textarabic{وَكَيْفَ تَصْبِرُ عَلَىٰ مَا لَمْ تُحِطْ بِهِ خُبْرًا}$$

And how can you have patience about a thing which you know not?

He meant, 'For I know that you will rightly condemn me, but I have knowledge of the wisdom of Allah and the hidden interests that I can see but you cannot.'

Since Moses (peace be upon him) does not have the knowledge that Allah gave to Al-Khidr (peace be upon him) therefore Moses (peace be upon him) cannot encompass everything that he will see when he follows Khidr (peace be upon him). It will be difficult for Musa to be patient since he (peace be upon him) does not know the purpose of the actions that Khidr will do. Moses (peace be upon him) would not be able to tolerate the extraordinary actions that Khidr would perform. He will not be able to be silent or express approval in the face of apparent evil. A person can be patient only if he has the knowledge and knows the purpose or the outcome of the action or the benefit of action.

# Verse 69

قَالَ

He said,

سَتَجِدُنِيٓ

"You will find me,

إِن

if

شَآءَ ٱللَّهُ

Allah wills,

صَابِرًا

patient,

وَلَآ

and not

أَعْصِى

I will disobey

لَكَ

your

أَمْرًا

order."

69

$$\text{قَالَ سَتَجِدُنِي إِن شَآءَ ٱللَّهُ صَابِرًا وَلَآ أَعْصِى لَكَ أَمْرًا} \quad ٦٩ \quad \text{[الكهف: 69]}$$

«[Moses] said, "You will find me, if Allah wills, patient, and I will not disobey you in [any] order." (69) » [Al-Kahf: 69]

$$\text{قَالَ}$$

(He said) meaning, Moses (peace be upon him) said:

$$\text{سَتَجِدُنِي إِن شَاءَ اللَّهُ صَابِرًا}$$

'If Allah wills, you will find me patient', with whatever I (Moses) see of your (Khidr) affairs,

$$\text{وَلَا أَعْصِي لَكَ أَمْرًا}$$

'And I will not disobey you in any order.' Meaning, 'I will not go against you in anything.'

Musa resolved to be patient, even before being put to the test. Musa said to Khidr, 'you will find me, patient, if Allah wills.' Musa believed that he (peace be upon him) would be able to be patient. But he attached this patience to the Will of Allah so that his patience would not be because of his pride or amazement about himself. This patience was something that Allah will bless him if He Wills. If Allah Wills then Musa will be patient.

Musa (peace be upon him) therefore promised Al-Khidr (peace be upon him) that he will be patient and will do what Khidr commands him to do and will stay away from what he prohibited.

قَالَ

He said,

فَإِنِ

"Then if

اتَّبَعْتَنِي

you follow me,

فَلَا

(do) not

تَسْـَٔلْنِي

ask me

عَن

about

شَيْءٍ

anything

حَتَّىٰ

until

أُحْدِثَ

I present

لَكَ

to you

مِنْهُ

of it

ذِكْرًا

a mention."

70

قَالَ فَإِنِ ٱتَّبَعْتَنِي فَلَا تَسْئَلْنِي عَن شَيْءٍ حَتَّىٰ أُحْدِثَ لَكَ مِنْهُ ذِكْرًا ﴿٧٠﴾

[الكهف: 70]

«He said, "Then if you follow me, do not ask me about anything until I make to you about it mention." (70) » [Al-Kahf: 70]

**Continuation of the Narration of the Prophet (peace and blessings of Allah be upon him)**

قَالَ فَمَا شَأْنُكَ قَالَ جِئْتُ لِتُعَلِّمَنِي مِمَّا عُلِّمْتَ رَشَدًا.
قَالَ أَمَا يَكْفِيكَ أَنَّ التَّوْرَاةَ بِيَدَيْكَ، وَأَنَّ الْوَحْيَ
يَأْتِيكَ، يَا مُوسَى إِنَّ لِي عِلْمًا لاَ يَنْبَغِي لَكَ أَنْ تَعْلَمَهُ

وَإِنَّ لَكَ عِلْمًا لاَ يَنْبَغِي لِي أَنْ أَعْلَمَهُ، فَأَخَذَ طَائِرٌ بِمِنْقَارِهِ مِنَ الْبَحْرِ وَقَالَ وَاللَّهِ مَا عِلْمِي وَمَا عِلْمُكَ فِي جَنْبِ عِلْمِ اللَّهِ إِلاَّ كَمَا أَخَذَ هَذَا الطَّائِرُ بِمِنْقَارِهِ مِنَ الْبَحْرِ

Al-Khidr said, "What do you want?' Moses said, 'I have come to you so that you may teach me of the truth which you were taught.' Al-Khidr said, 'Is it not sufficient for you that the Torah is in your hands and the Divine Inspiration comes to you, O Moses? Verily, I have a knowledge that you don't know, and you have a knowledge which I don't know.' At that time a bird took with its beak (some water) from the sea: Al-Khidr then said, 'By Allah, my knowledge and your knowledge compared to Allah's Knowledge is not more than what this bird has taken (the little water) with its beak from the sea.'

**Explanation of the Verse**

Khidr allowed Musa (peace be upon him) to follow him but set a condition that he should not ask anything. Khidr promised that he will explain and clarify his actions when the time is right.

This shows that the teacher can set his own rule and the one following him should obey. Musa was asked to be patient and to wait for Khidr's explanation that he will tell him at the appropriate time. Musa was asked to avoid asking questions or raising any objections.

This teaches us that when we are learning from a teacher that we should not be hasty in refuting the teacher but should wait for the teacher to explain it to him or wait till the issues become completely clear. This is from the manners of the student.

These restrictions put by Khidr was a test of Prophet Moses in the matter of attaining knowledge.

Our knowledge will be less when we don't follow the teacher. Musa asked questions and only learned the wisdom of the three actions of Khidr. If he had not asked, he would have learned much more. Patience is necessary when a person accompanies a scholar in his quest for knowledge. If there is no patience then he will lose many opportunities to gain additional knowledge. The more impatient a person is the greater his loss.

# Verse 71

فَٱنطَلَقَا

So they both set out

حَتَّىٰٓ

until

إِذَا

when

رَكِبَا

they had embarked

فِى

on

ٱلسَّفِينَةِ

the ship

خَرَقَهَا

he made a hole in it.

قَالَ

He said,

أَخَرَقْتَهَا

"Have you made a hole in it,

لِتُغْرِقَ

to drown

أَهْلَهَا

its people?

لَقَدْ

Certainly,

جِئْتَ

you have done

شَيْئًا

a thing

إِمْرًا

grave."

71

فَٱنطَلَقَا حَتَّىٰٓ إِذَا رَكِبَا فِى ٱلسَّفِينَةِ خَرَقَهَا قَالَ أَخَرَقْتَهَا لِتُغْرِقَ أَهْلَهَا لَقَدْ جِئْتَ شَيْئًا إِمْرًا ۝ [الكهف: 71]

«So they set out, until when they had embarked on the ship, al-Khidr tore it open. [Moses] said, "Have you torn it open to drown its people? You have certainly done a grave thing." (71) » [Al-Kahf: 71]

## Explanation of the Verse

Allah tells us that Moses and his companion Al-Khidr left after reaching an agreement and understanding. Al-Khidr had made it a condition that Musa should not ask him anything he found distasteful before Khidr initiated the discussion and offered an explanation. So, they boarded the ship which carried people from one shore to the other. The crew recognized Al-Khidr and let them ride aboard for free, in honor of Al-Khidr. When the boat took them out to sea and they were far from shore, Al-Khidr got up and damaged the boat, pulled out one of its planks, and patched it again with a piece of wood. Musa (peace be upon him) could not refrain from denouncing him, so he said:

$$\text{أَخَرَقْتَهَا لِتُغْرِقَ أَهْلَهَا}$$

"Have you damaged it wherein its people will drown?"

$$\text{لَقَدْ جِئْتَ شَيْئًا إِمْرًا}$$

Verily, you have committed a thing *Imr*.

Regarding *'Imr'*, Mujahid said: "An evil thing." Qatadah said, "An astounding thing."

Moses (peace be upon him) was not able to be patient because the actions of Khidr appeared outwardly to be something bad, for his actions caused damage to the boat which can lead to its passengers drowning. So Musa labeled this action as a dreadful action and disapproved it. He was not patient because Khidr's action was a major problem since the ship was ruined and could sink in the sea. Musa did not know Al-Khidr's intention. His (peace be upon him) objection was in accordance with the external appearance and was not out of place. He reacted to evil as any righteous servant of Allah would react under normal circumstances. He rebuked Khidr and told him about the harmful consequences of his action.

Musa himself was thrown into the river when he was a child. Anyone who saw his mother placing Musa in a wooden box and throwing him into the river would have thought that his mother was doing an evil thing if he did not have knowledge of why the mother of Musa was doing this action.

قَالَ

He said,

أَلَمْ

"Did not

أَقُلْ

I say,

إِنَّكَ

indeed, you

لَن

never

تَسْتَطِيعَ

will be able

مَعِيَ

with me

صَبْرًا

(to have) patience?"
72

قَالَ أَلَمْ أَقُلْ إِنَّكَ لَن تَسْتَطِيعَ مَعِيَ صَبْرًا ﴿٧٢﴾ [الكهف: 72]

«[Al-Khidr] said, "Did I not say that with me you would never be able to have patience?" (72) » [Al-Kahf: 72]

## Explanation of the Verse

When Musa (peace be upon him) denounced Khidr, Khidr said, 'Did I not tell you, that you would not be able to have patience with me?' He meant, 'this thing that I did deliberately is one of the things I said to you that you should not condemn me for because you do not know the whole story and there is a reason and a purpose for it that you do not know.' Khidr said that what has happened (the impatience of Musa) was what Khidr said would happen. Khidr reminded him of the condition which he had set for learning from him. This was a condition that Khidr knew Moses would be unable to keep.

# Verse 73

قَالَ

He said,

لَا

"(Do) not,

تُؤَاخِذْنِي

blame me

بِمَا

for what

نَسِيتُ

I forgot

وَلَا

and (do) not

تُرْهِقْنِي

be hard (upon) me

مِنْ

in

أَمْرِى

my affair

عُسْرًا

(raising) difficulty."

73

قَالَ لَا تُؤَاخِذْنِي بِمَا نَسِيتُ وَلَا تُرْهِقْنِي مِنْ أَمْرِي عُسْرًا ۝٧٣ [الكهف: 73]

«[Moses] said, "Do not blame me for what I forgot and do not cover me in my matter with difficulty." (73) » [Al-Kahf: 73]

## Continuation of the Narration of the Prophet (peace and blessings of Allah be upon him)

إِذْ أَخَذَ الْفَأْسَ فَنَزَعَ لَوْحًا، قَالَ فَلَمْ يَفْجَأْ مُوسَى إِلَّا وَقَدْ قَلَعَ لَوْحًا بِالْقَدُّومِ. فَقَالَ لَهُ مُوسَى مَا صَنَعْتَ قَوْمٌ حَمَلُونَا بِغَيْرِ نَوْلٍ، عَمَدْتَ إِلَى سَفِينَتِهِمْ فَخَرَقْتَهَا لِتُغْرِقَ أَهْلَهَا، لَقَدْ جِئْتَ شَيْئًا إِمْرًا. قَالَ أَلَمْ أَقُلْ إِنَّكَ لَنْ تَسْتَطِيعَ مَعِيَ صَبْرًا. قَالَ لَا تُؤَاخِذْنِي بِمَا نَسِيتُ وَلَا

تُرْهِقْنِي مِنْ أَمْرِي عُسْرًا، فَكَانَتِ الْأُولَى مِنْ مُوسَى نِسْيَانًا

Then suddenly Al-Khidr took an adze (similar to an axe) and plucked a plank, and Moses did not notice it till he had plucked a plank with the adze. Moses said to him, 'What have you done? They took us on board charging us nothing; yet you have intentionally made a hole in their boat so as to drown its passengers. Verily, you have done a dreadful thing.' Al-Khidr replied, 'Did I not tell you that you would not be able to remain patient with me?' Moses replied, 'Do not blame me for what I have forgotten, and do not be hard upon me for my fault.' So the first excuse of Moses was that he had forgotten.

**Explanation of the Verse**

Moses (peace be upon him) wanted to continue learning from Khidr (peace be upon him) and told him to not take him to account for forgetting. He realized his error. To forget is an acceptable excuse. This is similar to Musa (peace be upon him) not taking Yusha (peace be upon him) to account when he forgot to tell him about the fish. Moses also asked Khidr to be gentle and easy-going with him. Moses, therefore, admitted his error and asked Khidr to forgive him. Khidr pardoned him and allowed him to continue.

Musa forgot because the actions of Khidr were shocking to him. He thought Khidr was going to sink the boat while they were on it. This implies that a person may forget something when the events are shocking and severe.

The Prophet (peace and blessings of Allah be upon him) said, "Verily, Allah has excused my followers from genuine mistakes, forgetfulness, and what they have been forced to do."

# Verse 74

فَٱنطَلَقَا

Then they both set out

حَتَّىٰٓ

until

إِذَا

when

لَقِيَا

they met

غُلَـٰمًا

a boy,

فَقَتَلَهُ

then he killed him.

قَالَ

He said,

أَقَتَلْتَ

" Have you killed

نَفْسًا

a soul,

زَكِيَّةً

pure,

بِغَيْرِ

for other than

نَفْسٍ

a soul?

لَّقَدْ

Certainly,

جِئْتَ

you have done

شَيْــًٔا

a thing

نُكْرًا

evil."

74

فَٱنطَلَقَا حَتَّىٰٓ إِذَا لَقِيَا غُلَٰمًا فَقَتَلَهُۥ قَالَ أَقَتَلۡتَ نَفۡسًا زَكِيَّةَۢ بِغَيۡرِ نَفۡسٍ لَّقَدۡ جِئۡتَ شَيۡـَٔا نُّكۡرًا ﴿٧٤﴾ [الكهف: 74]

«So they set out, until when they met a boy, al-Khidr killed him. [Moses] said, "Have you killed a pure soul for other than [having killed] a soul? You have certainly done a deplorable thing." (74) » [Al-Kahf: 74]

## Explanation of the Verse

Al Khidr (peace be upon him) is teaching Moses (peace be upon him) about the decree of Allah. They may look evil from the outside but behind it is much mercy and goodness. The reason for his actions will be explained later by Al Khidr. Al Khidr is not doing anything out of his own will but by Allah's permission.

When Khidr killed a small boy who had done no wrong Moses became very angry. What evil could be greater than killing a small child for no apparent reason? This time Moses did not forget his promise but was not patient seeing what was according to him a great evil.

Destroying a ship cannot be compared to killing an innocent boy. This was something more evil and dreadful. Children have good actions written for them and their bad actions are not written against them, therefore they are innocent. A child before puberty is not held responsible even if he had killed someone. So what was the reason for Khidr to kill him? Moses asked impatiently even though Khidr had promised that he will explain everything later.

Moses, therefore, rebukes Khidr with a strong rebuke than Moses's previous admonishment with regards to the ship. In the case of the ship, the action of Khidr may or may not have caused drowning but in this case with the boy, the evil had already taken place.

# Verse 75

قَالَ

He said,

أَلَمْ

"Did not

أَقُل

I say

لَّكَ

to you

إِنَّكَ

that you,

لَن

never

تَسْتَطِيعَ

will be able

مَعِيَ

with me

صَبْرًا

(to have) patience?"

75

قَالَ أَلَمْ أَقُل لَّكَ إِنَّكَ لَن تَسْتَطِيعَ مَعِيَ صَبْرًا ۝ [الكهف: 75]

«[Al-Khidr] said, "Did I not tell you that with me you would never be able to have patience?" (75) » [Al-Kahf: 75]

## Explanation of the Verse

Al Khidr (peace be upon him) told Musa (peace be upon him) again that he won't be patient with him. This time he said it in a more severe way than the first time with a meaning that he had told him that he (Musa) will never be able to have patience with him (Khidr).

قَالَ

He said,

إِن

"If

سَأَلْتُكَ

I ask you

عَن

about

شَىْءٍ ۚ

anything

بَعْدَهَا

after it,

فَلَا

then (do) not

تُصَـٰحِبْنِي ۚ

keep me as a companion.

قَدْ

Verily,

بَلَغْتَ

you have reached

مِن لَّدُنِّي

from me

عُذْرًا

an excuse."

76

قَالَ إِن سَأَلْتُكَ عَن شَيْءٍ بَعْدَهَا فَلَا تُصَاحِبْنِي ۖ قَدْ بَلَغْتَ مِن لَّدُنِّي عُذْرًا ﴿٧٦﴾ [الكهف: 76]

«[Moses] said, "If I should ask you about anything after this, then do not keep me as a companion. You have obtained from me an excuse." (76) » [Al-Kahf: 76]

Musa (peace be upon him) said that if he asks him (Al Khidr) again then he should not accompany him. Musa blamed himself and did not blame his teacher.

This time Musa did not have any excuse. His reaction was not due to forgetfulness but genuine anger. Musa had agreed to not ask him about anything until it was explained to him but despite this, he had blamed Khidr twice.

Moses, therefore, said that Khidr may not accompany him if he asks him about anything after this as he has given him sufficient excuse to leave him.

The Prophet (peace and blessings of Allah be upon him) said, "May Allah have mercy upon us and upon Musa. If he had stayed with his companion (had he shown patience) he would have seen wonderful things, but he said, 'If I ask you anything after this, keep me not in your company, you have received an excuse from me'."

# Verse 77

فَٱنطَلَقَا

So they set out

حَتَّىٰٓ

until

إِذَآ

when

أَتَيَآ

they came

أَهْلَ

(to the) people

قَرْيَةٍ

(of) a town,

ٱسْتَطْعَمَآ

they asked for food

أَهْلَهَا

(from) its people,

فَأَبَوْاْ

but they refused

أَن

to

يُضَيِّفُوهُمَا

offer them hospitality.

فَوَجَدَا

Then they found

فِيهَا

in it

جِدَارًا

a wall

يُرِيدُ

(that) want(ed)

أَن

to

يَنقَضَّ

collapse,

فَأَقَامَهُ ۚ

so he set it straight.

قَالَ

He said,

لَوْ

"If

شِئْتَ

you wished

لَتَّخَذْتَ

surely you (could) have taken

عَلَيْهِ

for it

أَجْرًا

a payment."

77

فَٱنطَلَقَا حَتَّىٰ إِذَآ أَتَيَآ أَهْلَ قَرْيَةٍ ٱسْتَطْعَمَآ أَهْلَهَا فَأَبَوْاْ أَن يُضَيِّفُوهُمَا فَوَجَدَا فِيهَا جِدَارًا يُرِيدُ أَن يَنقَضَّ فَأَقَامَهُۥ قَالَ لَوْ شِئْتَ لَتَّخَذْتَ عَلَيْهِ أَجْرًا ۝٧٧ [الكهف: 77]

«So they set out, until when they came to the people of a town, they asked its people for food, but they refused to offer them hospitality. And they found therein a wall about to collapse, so al-Khidr restored it. [Moses] said, "If you wished, you could have taken for it a payment." (77) » [Al-Kahf: 77]

## Explanation of the verse

In this final incident, Khidr does something good to people who were not worthy. In the first two incidents, he had done something that appeared to be evil.

They reached a town and asked its people for food and hospitality. The people of the town however refused to accommodate them.

The Prophet (peace and blessings of Allah be upon him) said, "Whoever believes in Allah and the Last Day, let him honor his guest'. But in this town, they did not honor their guest and were deficient in their faith.

In this town, they found a wall that was about to fall. Khidr then set it up straight and fixed it. This was unusual since if someone was treated the way they were treated by the people of the town then he would have not cared about their wall and would have instead thought, 'let that wall fall'.

Musa (peace be upon him) wanted Khidr to take credit for his work of strengthening the wall and take wages for it. This time Musa did not blame him for building the wall but gently and kindly said that if Khidr had wished he could have taken wages for it. This was now the third time that Musa had questioned Khidr and had again failed to fulfill his promise of being patient, therefore Khidr had good reason to leave him.

Prophet Musa (peace be upon him) had said this because the people of that town did not deserve to be served in any way, since they had refused to feed the hungry travelers even for one time. Musa just wanted some compensation for repairing the wall so that they may buy some food and drink. He asked this question intentionally and this was not due to forgetting like the first time. But this was the third time and therefore this lead to the parting of ways between them.

# Verse 78

قَالَ

He said,

هَـٰذَا

"This

فِرَاقُ

(is) parting

بَيْنِي

between me

وَبَيْنِكَ ۚ

and between you.

سَأُنَبِّئُكَ

I will inform you

بِتَأْوِيلِ

of (the) interpretation

مَا

(of) what

لَمْ

not

تَسْتَطِعْ

you were able

عَلَيْهِ

on it

صَبْرًا

(to have) patience.

78

قَالَ هَـٰذَا فِرَاقُ بَيْنِي وَبَيْنِكَ سَأُنَبِّئُكَ بِتَأْوِيلِ مَا لَمْ تَسْتَطِع عَّلَيْهِ صَبْرًا ۝ [الكهف: 78]

«[Al-Khidr] said, "This is parting between me and you. I will inform you of the interpretation of that about which you could not have patience (78) » [Al-Kahf: 78]

**Explanation of the verse:**

Khidr reminded Musa that he had promised after the second incident of questioning that if he asked him anything after that then he would not accompany him any further. So, Khidr told that this is the parting of ways between them.

We should think about how many times we judged something prematurely and gave our views in a hurry or in anger without knowing the full story. When we are patient and hear both sides of an incident then we will learn more.

Musa (peace be upon him) was given three chances. This incident teaches us that we need to be patient and not comment or argue when we are learning from our teacher.

Al Khidr will now inform him of the interpretation of his three actions which Musa (peace be upon him) could not be patient about.

The Prophet (peace and blessings of Allah be upon him) said, "I wished that Musa could have remained patient so that Allah could have told us more about their story."

# Verse 79

أَمَّا

As for

ٱلسَّفِينَةُ

the ship,

فَكَانَتْ

it was

لِمَسَـٰكِينَ

of (the) poor people

يَعْمَلُونَ

working

فِي

in

ٱلْبَحْرِ

the sea.

فَأَرَدتُّ

So I intended

أَنْ

that

أَعِيبَهَا

I cause defect (in) it

وَكَانَ

(as there) was

وَرَآءَهُم

after them

مَّلِكٌ

a king

يَأْخُذُ

who seized

كُلَّ

every

سَفِينَةٍ

ship

غَصْبًا

(by) force.

أَمَّا ٱلسَّفِينَةُ فَكَانَتْ لِمَسَٰكِينَ يَعْمَلُونَ فِي ٱلْبَحْرِ فَأَرَدتُّ أَنْ أَعِيبَهَا وَكَانَ وَرَآءَهُم مَّلِكٌ يَأْخُذُ كُلَّ سَفِينَةٍ غَصْبًا ۝ [الكهف: 79]

«As for the ship, it belonged to poor people working at sea. So I intended to cause defect in it as there was after them a king who seized every [good] ship by force (79) » [Al-Kahf: 79]

Khidr said that he had damaged the ship to make it faulty because the king was an oppressor and seized every good and sound boat by force. So, Khidr wanted to prevent the king from taking this ship by making it appear faulty. By doing this the poor owners of the ship who had nothing else could benefit from it. Since their ship was damaged they were saved from having it taken by the king. Therefore, these poor people could easily repair their ship after the king had not seized it and continue to earn with the ship.

We, therefore, learn from this incident that we go through some kind of harm in our life so that we are protected from a greater harm. We should therefore always say 'alhamdulillah' (praise be to Allah), and be patient because in everything there is goodness. Even if some harm affects our livelihood, for sure in this there is protection from something greater.

Allah says in the Quran:

كُتِبَ عَلَيْكُمُ ٱلْقِتَالُ وَهُوَ كُرْهٌ لَّكُمْ وَعَسَىٰٓ أَن تَكْرَهُوا۟ شَيْـًٔا وَهُوَ خَيْرٌ لَّكُمْ وَعَسَىٰٓ أَن تُحِبُّوا۟ شَيْـًٔا وَهُوَ شَرٌّ لَّكُمْ وَٱللَّهُ يَعْلَمُ وَأَنتُمْ لَا تَعْلَمُونَ ۝ [البقرة: 216]

«Fighting has been enjoined upon you while it is hateful to you. But perhaps you hate a thing and it is good for you; and perhaps you love a thing and it is bad for you. And Allah Knows, while you know not. (216) » [Al-Baqara: 216]

The same principle is expressed in the Western proverb: "Every cloud has a silver lining." This incident also serves as the basis for explaining the purpose of evil in a world created by Allah. Allah did not create evil or allow evil to take place for evil itself, but He created evil for the good He knew it would produce. Nothing that Allah creates is completely evil. Every evil event has a good side for which it was created or allowed to happen.

It is knowledge of this reality about this world that gives believers the confidence to be patient in the most trying times.

The Prophet (peace and blessings of Allah be upon him) said, "The affair of the believer is amazing! The whole of his life is beneficial, and this is only in the case of the believer. When good times come to him, he is thankful and this is good for him. And when bad times befall him, he is patient and this is also good for him."

Al Khidr in this verse attributes the act of damaging the ship to himself by saying, "I wanted to cause a defect in it." This is so that a person avoids attributing evil directly to God.

وَأَمَّا

And as for

ٱلْغُلَـٰمُ

the boy

فَكَانَ أَبَوَاهُ

his parents were

مُؤْمِنَيْنِ

believers,

فَخَشِينَآ

and we feared

أَن

that

يُرْهِقَهُمَا

he would overburden them

طُغْيَـٰنًا

(by) transgression

وَكُفْرًا

and disbelief.

80

وَأَمَّا ٱلْغُلَـٰمُ فَكَانَ أَبَوَاهُ مُؤْمِنَيْنِ فَخَشِينَآ أَن يُرْهِقَهُمَا طُغْيَـٰنًا وَكُفْرًا ۝ [الكهف: 80]

«And as for the boy, his parents were believers, and we feared that he would overburden them by transgression and disbelief (80) » [Al-Kahf: 80]

**Explanation of the Verse**

The second incident is explained in this verse. This is regarding the loss of life which is not easy for anyone to face. But had this child remained alive then he would have taken himself and his family to the Hellfire. Thus a loss may take place in this life so that a person is saved from a greater trial and an eternal loss.

Allah is the All-Knower. He knows every possibility of what can happen in the future.

Allah will not burden a person more than what he can handle. The parents of this child who was killed were believers. They could handle the loss of the child with patience.

The parents with the loss of this child maintained their faith and then they gained a better righteous child. Thus all of them, including the child who was killed were in Paradise.

So, if we don't know the reason behind the Decree of Allah we will be quick to judge.

Had the boy grown then he would have transgressed and disbelieved. He would have forced his parents to disbelieve as well, either due to their love for him or other reasons. If he was not killed then all of them would have been afflicted and would be in eternal loss.

We should therefore have good thoughts about Allah and He is the Most Merciful.

This story consoles parents who have lost their children. Whoever loses their child then they should realize that their child is in paradise.

Abu Sinan said: "I buried my son Sinan and Abu Talhah Al-Khawlani was sitting on the rim of the grave. When I wanted to leave he took me by my hand and said: 'Shall I not inform you of some good new O Abu Sinan!' I said: 'Of course.' He said: 'Ad-Dahhak bin Abdur-Rahman bin Arzab narrated to me, from Abu Musa Al-Ash'ari: "The Messenger of Allah (peace and blessings of Allah be upon him) said: 'When a child of the slave (of Allah) died, Allah says to the angels: "Have you taken the fruits of his work." They reply: "Yes." So, He says: "What did My slave say?" They reply: "He praised you and mentioned that to You is the return." So, Allah says: "Build a house in Paradise for My slave, and name it 'the house of praise.'"

# Verse 81

فَأَرَدْنَآ

So we intended

أَن

that

يُبْدِلَهُمَا

would change for them

رَبُّهُمَا

their Lord,

خَيْرًا

a better

مِّنْهُ

than him

زَكَوٰةً

(in) purity

وَأَقْرَبَ

and nearer

رُحْمًا

(in) affection.

81

فَأَرَدْنَآ أَن يُبْدِلَهُمَا رَبُّهُمَا خَيْرًا مِّنْهُ زَكَوٰةً وَأَقْرَبَ رُحْمًا ۝ [الكهف: 81]

«So we intended that their Lord should substitute for them one better than him in purity and nearer to mercy (81) » [Al-Kahf: 81]

He wanted Allah to replace the boy with one who was more pure in the religion and better for his parents.

Even though the parents would not have seen the benefit of this Decree of Allah in this life, they will see the benefit of their loss on the Day of Judgement. They will know the Divine wisdom of the loss of their child on the Day of Judgment.

وَأَمَّا

And as for

ٱلْجِدَارُ

the wall,

فَكَانَ

it was

لِغُلَـٰمَيْنِ يَتِيمَيْنِ

for two orphan boys,

فِى

in

ٱلْمَدِينَةِ

the town,

وَكَانَ

and was

تَحْتَهُ

underneath it

كَنزٌ

a treasure

لَّهُمَا

for them

وَكَانَ

and was

أَبُوهُمَا

their father

صَـٰلِحًا

righteous.

فَأَرَادَ

So intended

رَبُّكَ

your Lord

أَن

that

يَبْلُغَآ

they reach

أَشُدَّهُمَا

their maturity,

وَيَسْتَخْرِجَا

and bring forth

كَنزَهُمَا

their treasure

رَحْمَةً

(as) a mercy

مِّن

from

رَّبِّكَ ۚ

your Lord.

وَمَا

And not

فَعَلْتُهُو

I did it

عَنْ

on

أَمْرِى ۚ

my (own) accord.

ذَٰلِكَ

That

تَأْوِيلُ

(is the) interpretation

مَا

(of) what

لَمْ

not

تَسْطِع

you were able

عَلَيْهِ

on it

صَبْرًا

(to have) patience."

82

وَأَمَّا ٱلْجِدَارُ فَكَانَ لِغُلَٰمَيْنِ يَتِيمَيْنِ
فِي ٱلْمَدِينَةِ وَكَانَ تَحْتَهُۥ كَنزٌ لَّهُمَا
وَكَانَ أَبُوهُمَا صَٰلِحًا فَأَرَادَ رَبُّكَ أَن
يَبْلُغَآ أَشُدَّهُمَا وَيَسْتَخْرِجَا كَنزَهُمَا
رَحْمَةً مِّن رَّبِّكَ ۚ وَمَا فَعَلْتُهُۥ عَنْ
أَمْرِى ۚ ذَٰلِكَ تَأْوِيلُ مَا لَمْ تَسْطِع
عَّلَيْهِ صَبْرًا ﴿٨٢﴾ [الكهف: 82]

«And as for the wall, it belonged to two orphan boys
in the city, and there was beneath it a treasure for
them, and their father had been righteous. So your
Lord intended that they reach maturity and extract
their treasure, as a mercy from your Lord. And I did it
not of my own accord. That is the interpretation of

that about which you could not have patience."(82)»
[Al-Kahf: 82]

## Explanation of the Verse

In this verse, we come to know the wisdom behind the third incident. Khidr had helped repair the wall that was about to collapse. He did this good action even though the townspeople were inhospitable. We should not stop doing good actions seeking a reward from the people, but we should do actions for the pleasure of Allah and seek a reward from Him.

There was a treasure under the wall. This belonged to two orphan boys whose father had died and their father was a righteous man.

Anyone who is righteous is a believer and Allah protects his children and the property of his children. The righteousness of the father had an effect even after his death. The father had left his children with a treasure and did not leave them poor. He did not want his children to face the trial of poverty.

Allah wanted to give the children this wealth when they were mature and not immediately since wealth when given to an immature youngster becomes a trial to him and he may waste it. Also, the people of the town were bad and if the children had got the treasure immediately then the town's people would have stolen the treasure.

A man once came to the Prophet (peace and blessings of Allah be upon him) and told him he wanted to give all his wealth in the cause of Allah, but the Prophet (peace and blessings of Allah be upon him) told him to leave at least a third for his children.

It does not negate *tawakkul* (reliance on Allah) when a person takes the means to leave wealth for their children.

If a person is righteous then Allah may send someone to save his offspring and wealth.

The children only got the wealth when they were mature and not earlier. This was for their benefit. Sometimes we wonder, 'Why did I not get this before?'. But the reason why we got something late is also a Mercy from Allah and from His wisdom.

Al Khidr (peace be upon him) did not do anything because he wanted to do it, rather it was by the Mercy of Allah and at His command.

Al Khidr explained all the three incidents and the reason why they occurred.

# Conclusion

From this story, we learn a number of lessons that have been explained in the explanation of the verses. To summarize we learn the following lessons:

1. The virtue of knowledge. We should even travel to seek it. Moses (peace and blessings of Allah be upon him) traveled a great distance and went through hardship for the sake of learning knowledge.

2. One should prioritize increasing one's own knowledge. We should then teach others what we have learned.

3. We can hire a servant so that the servant can take care of one's needs and we can have time to rest and relax.

4. We should inform the servant and travel companions about the purpose of the travel and our aim and destination. This will make them fully prepare for the journey.

5. We should feed the servant the food that we eat and we should eat together.

6. The seeker of knowledge should address his teacher in a gentle manner. He should show humility to the teacher and express his need for the knowledge that the teacher has.

7. A person should attribute knowledge to Allah and give thanks to Allah for having blessed him with knowledge.

8. Beneficial knowledge is that which guides us to righteous actions.

9. If a person is not patient to accompany a scholar and learn from then he misses out on gaining a great deal of knowledge.

10. One should not be hasty in passing a judgment concerning any matter until one knows the aim behind it and the goal that is sought.

11. A greater evil may be warded off by a lesser evil. A greater interest may be served by foregoing a lesser interest.

# Bibliography:


1. Tafseer Ibn Katheer.

2. Tafseer As-Saadi.

3. Tafseer Soorah al-Kahf Shaikh Muhammad al-Uthymeen.

4. Tafseer Soorah al-Kahf Dr. Abu Ameenah Bilal Philips

5. The Lit Cave from Surah al-Kahf

www.ingramcontent.com/pod-product-compliance
Lightning Source LLC
Chambersburg PA
CBHW030332160726
47992CB00005B/2245